of rain and nettles wove

# of rain and nettles wove

gillian parrish

Singing Horse Press 2018

of rain and nettles © 2018 by Gillian Parrish. All rights reserved. Except for brief quotations in critical articles or reviews, this book may not be reproduced, in whole or in part, by any means, without written permission from the publisher and the copyright holder.

ISBN 978-0-935162-60-8

Singing Horse Press
12170 Ragweed Street
San Diego, CA 92129

Singing Horse Press books are available from the publisher at singinghorsepress.com or from Small Press Distribution (800) 869-7553 or at www.spdbooks.org.

acknowledgments

The author thanks the journals in which some of these poems have appeared.

American Letters & Commentary "so that we can say it in our own voices"

Cimarron Review "in which she speaks of surrounding or intermediate powers"

Gulf Coast "this destiny is getting out of control"

Hayden's Ferry Review "palinodes"

The Literary Review "tilth"; "might come to rest"

Missouri Review "first offering"

Phoebe "from the book of mortal parts"; "transmission"

Spinning Jenny "momentary gods"

U City Review "february"

Volt "in which we speak of the global marketplace"; "forager"

And with gratitude for many friends and teachers along the way. The book is for them and for all of us in between.

contents

from the book of mortal parts   11
in which she speaks of surrounding
   or intermediate powers   13
so that we can say it in our own voices   14
inner mongolia   16
in which we speak of the global marketplace   17
momentary god   18
welter of stems   19
palinodes   21
flowers fall   22
momentary god   33
burning glass   34
if the line of the heart is chained or jagged   39
tilth   40
forager   41
first offering   46
what is given   47
transmission   48
and this is how we think anything is better nothing   49
momentary god   50
first task   51
this destiny is getting out of control   53
and now i will be light blue   56
midwinter   57
with the static possibilities of storms   58
fairings   59
householder   65
hand on the gate   66
might come to rest   67
february   72
notes   73

'The rain comes, there is rest.'

—*I Ching*

from the book of mortal parts

cloud-suck'd   bustle   to shadow: the flimsy streets
                    a sea

in the book   in the sky
behold   such glittering ships
such tongue   and flicker
crow scrawl & starling

out the window   the day
breaks into white sycamore

bewilderment, my rooms—& wilder
streets in bloom
in singing blood

the caveat : my body
column of chatter   column of water
these bruised bones   these bruised streets

might
winnow
and shine

but where can i rest?

if the streets are water

and the tongue is a blunder

i found late sky and bells
  these rented rooms

and the leaf light on the walls is also water

and the throat is the dark *in the dark of the dark*

sometimes   my body knows
  the sudden flesh   inside
the church bells   the empty   the emptying
  sound
between

in which she speaks of surrounding or intermediate powers

many things happened in parking lots
(fifteen summers in a katydid yell)

having weathered a club and other weathers
took my car   drove it

an idea of finding hidden treasure
somewhere between the Safeway and the dockyard

to the tune of pirate radio
waiting for America to rain

an idea of instinctive ceremony
bones meant faultlessness   lions meant fire

knew there would be fortune in movement
took my car   broke it in places

there are circles of light on the causeways
what was asked was what we came for

in the secondhand stores in the bar rooms in the libraries of
   the capitol
there were circles of light

certain rites happened without knowing it
and i waited for lilies to remake the river

bone means nothing sticks   lion means enough
(here in my faded summer dress)

so that we can say it in our own voices

'In the city, they stood   on a bridge   i think,
   over a cold river'
in ashes   in dog-skin   in winter
green neon lights on the water

said, 'i will listen,'
   then thought it might be very hard
midnight.   wanting nothing they knew

make a place to sit down.   tell the part
about the ~~needles~~ nettles   and the faraway cup
call it her call it this call it a given
amiss   *this fathoms-deep body*

and if i must be
 'haply'   made beggar   made prince 'to find her
again at the world's end   in a palace of glass
in a wood   beyond the sea'

'machine made of salt,' said the drowned girl
seven years later   *you know what to make*
 rooftops juniper blue, the taste of rainwater
it might cost,   it might cost her

'Subhuti,   What do you think?'   (hand on the gate)
'world merely
 called world'
why then should we be disconsolate?

i mean what the fuck is wrong with you
stood for a while in the pines
 'Love   has not been learned'   (the gesture

of glass   the gesture of flowers   the gesture of pollution)
'three portions of blood-red moss'
(and this will make you happy)
but i   blacked out my eyes
went south   lodestar : dissembler.

clinic said my heart was alright
the ice is breaking in the trees the trees are breaking
the nowhere   the lure   the forest   the dogs
'Subhuti, why is it?'   thought : mountain   thought about

the ~~dream~~ green of its former skin
  and that was an end.   *stood for a while*
           on a bridge   i think
in the pinewoods   dreamt the dark awake

city not a city but a mountain—*i would not go back*
the world ripening around them
through numberless gates they passed
'where she sat "weaving" and "crying"'

the tears of a hundred   ~~choose~~ chose
gesture of stem   gesture of stem   the day
cannot be far away
from which we started

'for a long time I ~~yearned~~ learned to be useless'
 like a faraway field   'that may be likened to the rain'
so what the fuck   if I must be   *mistook*
       'of rain and nettles wove'

thus this very crowned 'adornment': *gesture*
(of flowers)   *that casts less shadow*
'and may you get it,' said the fox,
who thereupon entered the river

inner mongolia

And how did you get there?

goatskin and twine

lights ripening overhead

thru static and gorges
i passed

'intending only
to pick violets'

What did you do there exactly?

studied the
colors
(kingfisher,
qualm)

learned shapes for 'between'
and 'remedy'
and 'this'

Why did you run?

for lost devotion
is daylight's crawl
thru the fuzzbox
of a single room
(marigold, black fly)

in which we speak of the global marketplace

it's not so different this tree and the one outside you

or the sea and a cat with eyes like the sea

the book said 'rely on your own place like a friend'

wind rimed with coconut   dried palm   and brine

he said   *lost five of my beautiful years*   leaned back

river light loose on the ceiling   running

said *hotels buried the headland   buried the headland*

to one born somewhere long-buried

'bodies letters hearts tongues and eyes'

O resinous Lady   did you see it

the differences you see are circumstantial

to be born where most of the trouble is what you make

the bright feet of their Lady gold-clad behind glass

their glass lanterns   their black boats along the shore

paint eyes on the prow against drowning

the sounds of other ships and we can only

momentary god

(5th hexagram)

the pigeon I carry between my lungs
pearl welter my winter yard
and cupboards unclosed
we wait and wait

a welter of stems drawn freehand

'took him as talisman'   spent

half my life   watching for rain

'how will you begin?'

my linden-crook'd dowsing rod
my flesh arms and i *and i*

  thought myself

         a
   forgotten
   bell

threshold—

  stopped on the stairs   looking out

   a habit of exile
          'mere hull' 'mere quiver'

and the awful blank of my palms

but oh   the windows

winterkill   the park ugly with mud
seven stone ponies   broken-footed   blind
                                       mica-bright

and the children growing old in low-fi
when they run they run in voices

  each
daybreak: white sycamore
  like some bright rescue

how will i be
  the lookout

palinodes

I. Fuck the Pandas

I never went in to see who played. In the market stalls
I never bought the cloud-dark eggs.
Nor the cakes of tea that curl in the palm.

II. Fuck the Pandas

I never went in to see who played.
In the market stalls I never bought
the cloud-dark eggs. Nor anise
flowers. Nor meat. My mouth
all thumbs and shards.

III. Fuck the Pandas

No kung fu courtyards;
not even clouds scrolling by.

No bread no milk no winter.
Not a friend for nine thousand miles.

IV. Fuck the Pandas

Yellow plums white plum flowers along a stone wall.
My haircut so ugly and my big velcro shoes.

And what did we leave there my darling.

flowers fall

"Springfield": Chi-Chi's American flag parking lot,
                                                    K-mart
red neon in a white sky,   sirens

blowing in from the highway—

                    Looked.

Saw each other.
Laughing.

but garlands
                    processions

        and mirrors of jade

when Chuck died   on the stairs
near the end   of the book   i read to you
about a boy   moving through time   it was a story

i loved as a child   you would have been
eleven   your AC/DC shirt   your fear

       we were children together   faraway
                            and we lived
on cabbages   on rice and black pepper
it was pigs   it was   a green river   and the words

there broke my mouth   but in our little room   our own
no longer came in colors   came apart
                                   tho i read to you
on a bed   beneath a nicotine ceiling
with our shins pressed together we cried
when Chuck died   when his head

                like blood
                        and berries
            (burning copper smells)

            there were marigolds   strung low
                        below lintels

            the wooden courtyards

            blankets afloat in the windows
            children in the windows

                        thresholds
                    lit with rice
                        petals   dung
                        and vermillion

              hey

                    little brother, little brother

                how we walked there

suddenly   weird

dog sounds   my mouth

                         is full of tea flowers

at the end of sixteen seasons

                                        'conditions of the roads
                                          and a vow to fulfill'

                    i had no idea what any of this meant

                                                    'to marry':
                                                the whole great
                                              undertow—gone
                                            to the fathers gone
                                               to the mothers

                         sorry means *hurry or blossom or go*

                                          and what am i?
                                         blackened copper.

                                      an airplane window
                         crowded with snow mountains
                               on the Delmar bus east

St. Louis and i keep dreaming
a big messy movie they call 'Asia' dreaming floods
dreaming dogs   it was messy   you were
                        something   like home
               i dream
                    in blue. in blue
                               and carnelian
river smells and the shell-colored light of an oracle sky

full moon eaten moon and what we came for
and the little black dog that followed you home

as a child

thought about books and endings   thought about rain
and the owl living under the rooftiles

   years

  years

the radial possibilities of you

        blue of blue

  inside these rented rooms

                    and what are you?

                         shadow of glass

                         shadow of water

                         but we suffer

rode a bus south
woke: it was wheatfields
and you were my friend

long white road and an oxcart
we rode looking back

at the mountain
we climbed in the dark

6:00   we passed
a monk on the empty road
the muscles of his calves   ordinary,
                              walking
      beat a drum
     between steps
            he walked   thru the cold
       green morning

     barefoot
    toward Vulture Peak

'yellow plums white plum flowers along a stone wall'

momentary god

(56th hexagram)

dog in my back
scraped knuckles   my flesh eyes
the nightfalls
and streets and all strangers

burning glass

      'unmark'd'
        my blue boy

   where we
        slept

wishes
the last word from you

and the floor for a while
was land-under-the-waves

when i stood up
sky so yellow
in the west
and the black trees

there are chicken bones under the gingkos

under the gingkos women gather yellow plums

(tho there is no one i wish for)

for the book said i was not ready

'the voice was feeble
and the nuptial cup—'

noon was not what we thought
black birds tracing the edges of the outer world

and what is night but space for breathing, broken
crockery, dry riverbed, the fine white light
 of high deserts

and always you were the path
between the trees

nearly cover to cover in this
book of ghosts and mountains
but the gates of winter are closing

'if the line of the heart is chained or jagged'

'something false appeared and passed away'
defined by its hinges   found wanting

drawing lines between pulse and desire
mixing footfall and rain

in and out and in and
i am sidewalk scrying

in the blur of six o'clock blue
wanting dominion   wanting to be used up

my heart my reflexive stutter
drawn between peacock and bone

is asking what it covets   what is enough
is eating its emerald skin

tilth

This was supposed to be about a field.

Whenever I see 'supposed'
I see milk-white ceramic hands.

The field would've favored production: rows
of marl and pleated green. A harrow and 'we
sprinkle in the seeds.' I suspect

you are suspicious. The backstory gussied up.
I suspect ease and 'this time' and my motives.
The field to be called The End

of Trying. Told my messed up arm the deal—how softly
the turnstiles—'then we weed and protect it.'

Misgivings, their tines all flapped away.

forager

        cut bloom from blackness
        and farther   darkly daughter
        (what would you be like?)

away and away and away

took footfall ~~my body~~

took briar took sleet

ten thousand miles

across mountains

                              for luck for sacred
                        alphabets the peaks on fire

feeling for embers
(this is an ember)

~~lone~~ long in the dark
morning the bad time
        with bird cry—

daybreak: light
of my eyes   (i thought i
was inside my eyes)

wandered far
in a cast-off coat
the very green the wild green of peacock—

'and thus did we waste and exhaust our hearts,
 and thus did we exhaust our hearts'

                         for undone is half begun
                         in a manner of speaking

                              if speaking is a torch
                                 instead of night

my cask of thorn my golden egg
my spur my burning house my bright keel —

                                        a body is but eros and erosion
                                              in all the old stories

                                        and what would you make of it?

meadow *meadow* *meadow*

first offering

road along the bottomlands
snow melt and still
jack-knifed truck in a ditch
when it comes she said *there is nothing you can do*
it's gonna take you
so many old wooden houses
grown over in wild vines the ground
a silver fire of mown corn
one day you will have to let go of everything
and what can help you
is it the wide fields the dark eyes of the deer
i have been awful things
i have been the light falling
over us the wing beat of vultures
of swans from the north
where the road crosses over the water

what is given

side by side into the wind she says
you always were my daughter
and we step into the wood to the sea

the white path
thru the pines

breaks to blue;
'the space between'
 she said, and small
        the blue

shadows in the glitter
   of the dunes

all the tall
grasses lit
gold to let go of

a gift i choose:
 the storm-
  tossed roots
make a door
 of the sky

transmission

Across the river the fields have deepened and dried to a darker green. No longer empty, flecked with bent backs in blue cotton, the rows croon with April's issue: cabbage sheen and the lean white stars of pepper blossoms. Next time we'll pay attention, see how each changed thing advances. Time is scarce, and we ride it down with idiot dogs. There should be strainers in the gutters to catch its brittle scat, its lacquered relics. We hustle around in our hard little boots trying to map the world. We whisper *dumb luck* and *done time*. How can we occupy what we cannot say—cut sage, the flexing light on the mountains? The river is bottle-green. It's nearly the turquoise stream from your pictures, your toes ghost blur at the edges. How do we all go under? Taste dies on the tongue; every touch is a crossing over. We live inside an hour here, a thin skin, a minute, a powder of tinted currents and cleft fields. We can't hold things very long, but our strung plants and blistered hands might mean we're living. Watch out, the world's behind you, and nothing's holding anything, and the word's a curled wing in the dark. Across the river, they've drowned in the messy tripods of their bean plants. A moth toddles past in the wind. The switch grass hooks the sun. Over the river, they move in their staked fields. The river is green like your eyes were. Everything is a tumbled procession. And we stand here in our hunger boots trying.

and this is how we think anything is better than nothing

morning sycamore i'll miss
this white waking to brightness

and it took some time to learn to be alone
in the mornings i woke
breathing thin panes of glass

thought 'sycamore' thought
the-cracked-wild-white of its branches:
'daylight' in this dissolving world

momentary god

(48th hexagram)

the child that breathes inside my throat,
mock daylight my little reed
and the sink weighted with water—
we lean to meet

first task

'finding a flower
in a graveyard she
should bind it in her hair'

 begun it

     gardens

(having hid the wilderness
in the home)

and i will be the maze the maid
the minotaur the thread—tho i will not be led
and i don't know the way

there are things i want to learn what can i learn here

pathwork of root and stem: worlds
that we don't have words for
set the boundaries (mark
the narrow rows by hand)

there's a field inside my body
where i listen in the grass
and thus have i heard the falling
rain on the wind the seeds of no color
'sometimes it's heaven
when you look at things'

     all the edges
  and angles
on which birds can sit
lay out the offerings
(tree-full of starlings)
'and there was never any reason
to be so unhappy' turn back to my work

of worry weave through the night and lead
me deep sun treasure house the pollen path
and the grass is time
the fields burning and ripening
half-made wet awake world
fill out the black bowl

this destiny is getting out of control

I was making/I was building

cold rain and a window make a sheer spring
and the streets at last resemble simplicity
the black trees wet and green diagonals

 another Sunday eaten by doubt
 its extra eyes its peacock glaze

in the park the feeble grass an asinine green
the likes of me and what i want is to be more
like the new-rinsed fences and river sounds of buses passing

'hurry up,' said the ceiling

use the word 'homemade'
and 'precept' and 'portion'

am i learning to love
how things are
(as much as they are)   the slow
eyes of our eyes we might call trust

in the empty park in the nightfall in the april
in the rainy park   the swings
hang in straight lines

from my window the blue
seats like the pelts of dependable maritime animals
the park is a simple place   it sits

what lies in the pines

amnesiac parking lots

what has been cast

      bent in two half the nights
        sorting seeds

i'm not reading   thinking about a green river
moon falling half the night through the tree

      each thing resembled only itself

tho this april smells the same cold green
as the gardenhose water of august (tho in april
i long for april) tho there's nowhere to sit here and where
are the children tho happenstance tho avarice tho rue—

  the swings wild in the park
  but the fingers need not grip, for

      greenly

          the daffodils
          'happened'

this flower

so many seeds
nothing is lost

and the little grasses
   that don't need us

      (tho
    it is
     a garden)

in the park the kids are swinging
leaning into what's here

and now i will be light blue

it was then

  came through the branches
the wide sky   immaculate

no more to be stored no more to be got
the plowed the seeded fields

we'd thrown bright coins
so many times

and the rains still came with the leaves

said   what then   what then
    but this—her eyes cool lakelight

          bespoken:

the rinsed streets   the gates
and the daffodils broadcasting blankness
and the night

said it happens when your eyes lapse

said it happens

the fields just starting to shine

midwinter

(for Gene)

white sun i cannot speak
wild inside the black trees

red sun our only hill
is a highway towards the sunset you

talk about the fire beyond the trees
my body is a burning house

along the highway wildfire windows
tell me that the dark is falling

like some days how the light is
and you be my poem

with the static possibilities of storms

'a hundred mothers kind'

first star between the power lines

i wish for you

silver strikes violet strikes red glass and green

resembling silence

the eye is a clear place

in a bamboo grove lit with cat piss   crickets' broken-chalk
                                                                                   chimes

in the grass   their bright splintered breathing

in the dark   *not a cloud not a cloud not a cloud*

forms: 1-3 fair, 4-5 feire, feyre, 4-7 faire, fayre, 5-6 fayer (6 faier), 7 fare

fairing (n):

1. Of the weather: To clear; esp. with "away"
2 a. A gift given at or brought from a fair, often assoc. with courtship
    b. transf. A free-given gift of any kind

fairing (v): To make fair; to make clean; to beautify

fare (n):
1.   a. A going, journeying; course, passage, way; voyage
       b. A road, track (obs.)
2. a. A passage or excursion for which a price is paid; hence b. Cost of conveyance; passage money
3. a. The passenger, or (now rarely) company of passengers
    b. The 'load' (of an animal). The cargo of a vessel; a load or 'catch' of fish
4. A certain game at dice

fare (v1):
1. intr. To journey, travel, make one's way.
2. to go astray
3. a. of persons, lit. to let fare: = to let go.
    b. To flow, 'run'. Of immaterial things, esp. time: To go, pass, proceed.
    c. impersonal: To 'go'; to happen; to turn out. Occas. with well, ill, etc.
4. To 'go', pass, change into something else

fairings

listen   find your own way back
tho 'this pipe has a sorrowful tune' (and there
is no returning) such cliffs
such white cliffs and black
in the clover (loved
as a child)—but *hush*
for this is a night flight
'loaded deep across the seas'
 towards that old promise,
  that green
          'pavilion
where it always rains'

feathers-on-the-water
  and the bell starts
beech roots like rivers
   the westward leaning trees
what has been kept: mere

for the fare is dear here
and the market's bound
by 'one of the hollow paths'
the forgotten roads of the city

nowhere misled
        though led a long wild way
'by youths by maidens fair' old world
i've hurried to in glimpses green
and clear and fast and cold
seascapes in the moss
 'and the pale roses'
 in the sunken garden

those little girls
who eat the green thorns, (such dangers
growing up inside their skin)

'with just this paper for my passage'
bring me home

yes   (this young young place)
dockleaf
   for the pockets
for the nettle

       and tell
      the bluebells

i was away so long
  so long
 since i have heard
   such singing

three stone steps in the grass
             'alas,'

written on a packet
of bright-colored money
    london, 1983

look at the mustard fields
  sliding—and the green
she told me, 'you live on page 62'
the sudden dark heart
 of clover (small
   and demented)

for i cannot hold
headlands i cannot hold

  not wood nor water

through the wall they talk in voices
that are old songs

say what's missing
in your own tongue, your
old tongue, where bewilderment
meant plenty,
        'and with these golden
dragon coins to cast' (deep in wishes
  through the oaks), once
              lost, if lost
       if pixy-led
hold the mirror before you
throw the comb back behind
(and the greenwood's growing wilder
and the day is fickle-fair)
count your paces to the holy well

and of course the sea is also a mirror
'so sing, siren, for thyself'
of white lights in the water
of dark that makes the sparkling water

where things fast change shape, become
belly-soft, float white
  disappear

in the musicks of my inner ear
              abide
       my timbril fibril
                  lo
'where green waves flare
beneath the backs of crows'

where the black rocks
where the sweetest singing
  took my skin

and he said,
take me to your house
           if you can

(tho my heart
was of thorn)

felt for the road
by roundabouts

'three turns
to the garden gate'
where i pulled flowers

you stood in the garden
so patiently

i would give you the red red rose
all the ribbons of the fayre
to be your pinafore girl
in petticote in plimsole
fairing 'the first blood'

but this is not a rough sea this
mirror that we lean towards

said, 'you are the perfect weather' heavy clouds
traced with light, *trace out my*

salt-sea tangle lines to pocket
pieces of the land: thyme from the hilltop

the schoolyard   rolled to a stone
under the sea

'lost my name over the water'
the flowers that i looked for, for no

you cannot buy bluebells, at the gate
they took the seeds

take this silver
for my passage back 'where
i used to play on the green, where
all the hills echoed' (tho from there
i don't know the way) but beautiful

this half-finished thing—'(grave
the sentence deep),' listen
so the rain slows, listen
there is no other time

in this white circle of lamplight
take the nettles i have carried

'own wove   own wold
            greenly kept,'

and you hear me
under the words

that come belly to throat and in this
white rented bed in this
cottage crossed by salt paths

*close my eyes
and see bluebells*

under the lamplight
you flood my mouth

householder

new tree to learn

and the idea of home
rests on a door
of pressed pine

                                        wd 'forsake the world'
                                        wd 'dwell in the wood'

                                              but it's not a wood

                                        just dust the streets
                                      so dirty ghost dogs
                            the ghost and hungry children
                              ghost idea of white mountains
                      the trash-heap empty lots on fire

                                             how will i go
                                        where i'm going

                              'play-woman,' 'pilgrim'

hand on the gate

took the long way

the moon going down

and yellow windows

dreaming children 'mind

like a flower' the brick house

dog at the mercy

of an empty yard the years running

but as if spelled backwards flooding

the streets 'in wind, in rain'

at the mercy

'i have not given comfort'

only gifts that come easy

inside of bright paper

have not found happiness

'at the great festivals'

nor listened under the words

(every pulse is a seed)

i have not laid out the reddest fruits

sage who has sung past all desire

might come to rest

'in dog-skin
          slept'
  & white mouthful
 of lilies' (it was a story
i loved as a child)

 tell it,   midnight
    and what can be true
        of a body   'strewn across the plain'
in bloom   *in bloom*   in blood-red moss
   and the clear water   'for the terrible cup'

  for the tongue
believes it must be difficult
    back of the teeth   "blooded"
 'the things we want become like mad dogs barking'
half-fed   *so that no one else*

'this monster is quite honest'
fistfuls of rice   in the roots of the pine
   my tourniquet my heart my crown of envy
(her owl face her face of flowers)
 and the dancers just walk on their knees

 'for three years she sees nothing'
            fistfuls of rain-dark hair
    studied grudge
                        the ghost river
'for upon the charnel ground is built the palace'
  though she would deal hard for the dead

what is this spell upon me
i said something about the ~~dreams~~ rains
and i must go inside,
said the young woman softly
          in dog-skin slept
as if asleep

'what you need,' said the fox,
what you hide what you find
   ~~cruel~~ cool as a wish   a cup
of partless water   passed through the dark
 become it   (your child face
your face of jade) 'this fathoms-deep
body'

there would be many hesitations
   (far and far)   there would be dross
 scribbled girlish my dogheart
but to ford the black river—
                rue. and a kiss
  'there is no spell upon you'
begin to ask what fills your mouth

'how i never wanted to be this woman'
    law of the small   the green
              stems
so you must make it, said the fox, to
   the isle of the dead
and the well there   (as if there)
   ~~one day~~ on a day you will bring rain

but did we plan our plans—and did we linger
over ~~love and meat and~~ doubtful things
(half-curst be all wanderers)   three lifetimes
fled floods   in your own turning   *oh the*
              birds i followed west—
'cut away piece by piece'
   even then i was free

'and how should i regard my dreaming?'
my sow face my face of famine my face
of faraway my face of ought
my boy face my face of laurel of lily of dog's eye
of no-more-yearning of pearl
                     the ground

pushing up
through me
(secrets i learned from saints)
ford the river by trapped light   'by half-light blest'
by loosed skins by tendril   *crossed*
to the green isle   made
of myself   a well

february

                                        in the sidewalk grass
                                          two knuckles deep
                                              windshield glass
                                    color of a mountain lake

Notes

'the rain comes, there is rest' comes from Wilhelm and Baynes's translation of the *I Ching*. It appears in the commentary of hexagram number 9, "The Taming Power of the Small," a fitting sign for poems and fields to be tended. Stephen Karcher translates this line as 'There is *already* rain, and you already abide...'

"so that we can say it in our own voices" contains phrases adapted from Marie-Louise Von Franz's *Redemption Motifs in Fairytales* and John Crowley's *Engine Summer*. The blood-red moss is from a Scottish folk tale. The phrase 'this fathoms-deep body' is adapted from the *Rohitassa Sutta* from the Pali canon ("In this fathom-long body with its perceptions and thoughts there is the world, the origin of the world, the ending of the world and the path to the ending of the world"). References to Subhuti are adaptations from A.F. Price and Wong Mou-lam's translation of the *Diamond Sutra*.

"momentary god" is a term coined by German comparative religion scholar Hermann Usener in his book "names of gods" *Götternamen*, (1896). The term refers to a "god" (perhaps a force, perhaps a pattern of conditions) appearing for the duration of a single moment, in a particular place, fulfilling a specific purpose. The poems' form follows Eluard's "The River."

"tilth" is indebted to my father, who wrote to me of the power of marl and oyster shells in the process of planting the fields.

"this destiny is getting out of control" contains an echo of Basho's poem about Kyoto and Duncan's "Pindar" poem.

"forager" includes the line 'and thus did we waste and exhaust our hearts' from Fenollosa and Pound's *The Noh Theatre of Japan*.

"transmission" includes a line from "Sunday Morning" by the Velvet Underground.

the title "in which the line of the heart is chained or jagged" is adapted from a 19th century palmistry book *Your Luck's In Your Hand,* found at that old treasure-trove, Pilgrim's Books in Kathmandu.

"fairings" opens with definitions from the OED. The poem contains an adaptation of Shakespeare's "sing siren for thyself" from *The Comedy of Errors,* as well as three lines from Blake: From *Songs of Innocence* comes "Where I used to play on the green," from the poem "The Garden of Love"; the phrase "all the hills echoed," is from "The Nurse's Song"; "(Grave the sentence deep)" is from "Little Girl Lost," in *Songs of Experience.*

"householder" includes 'play-woman' from William LaFleur's chapter on the inn as symbol of the body in his study of medieval Japanese poetry, *The Karma of Words.*

"might come to rest" contains the line 'this monster is quite honest,' from Anthony C. Yu's translation of *Journey to the West.* 'And the dancers just walk on their knees' are choreographer Anna Sokolow in *The Vision of Modern Dance.* 'You will bring rain' is from Stephen Karcher's translation of the *I Ching,* hexagram 5, "Waiting."

Gillian Parrish spent some early years in the UK, some later ones in China and South Asia, and now lives in the brick and sycamore city of St. Louis, where she studied at Washington University and teaches as an assistant professor at Lindenwood University. She is the mothership of spacecraftproject, a journal that features interviews with artists and new work by poets from around the world.

Singing Horse Press Titles

Charles Alexander, *Near Or Random Acts*. 2004, $15.00
Charles Alexander, *At the Edge of the Sea*, 2018, $19
David Antin, *John Cage Uncaged Is Still Cagey*. 2005, $15.00
Rae Armantrout, *Collected Prose*. 2007, $17.00
Rachel Tzvia Back, *A Messenger Comes*, 2012, $15.00
Norman Fischer, *Success*. 1999, $14.00
Norman Fischer, *I Was Blown Back*. 2005, $15.00
Norman Fischer, *Questions/Places/Voices/Seasons*. 2009, $16
Norman Fischer, *The Strugglers*, 2013, $15.00
Norman Fischer, *Magnolias All At Once*, 2015, $15
Phillip Foss, *The Ideation*. 2004, $15.00
Phillip Foss, *Imperfect Poverty*. 2006, $15.00
Phillip Foss, *The Valley of Cranes*. 2010, $15.00
Mary Rising Higgins, *)cliff TIDES((*. 2005, $15.00
Mary Rising Higgins, *)joule TIDES((*. 2007, $15.00
Lindsay Hill, *Contango*. 2006, $14.00
Lindsay Hill, *The Empty Quarter*. 2010, $15.00
Karen Kelley, *Her Angel*. 1992, $7.50
Karen Kelley, *Mysterious Peripheries*. 2006, $15.00
Hank Lazer, *The New Spirit*. 2005, $14.00
Hank Lazer, *N18 (Complete)*. 2012, $15
Andrew Mossin, *The Epochal Body*. 2004, $15.00
Andrew Mossin, *The Veil*. 2008, $15.00
Paul Naylor, *Playing Well With Others*. 2004, $15.00
Gil Ott, *Pact*. 2002, $14.00
Rochelle Owens, *Hermaphropoetics*, 2017, $15
Ed Roberson, *The New Wing of the Labyrinth*. 2009, $15
Ted Pearson, *Encryptions*. 2007. $15.00
Ted Pearson, *Extant Glyphs: 1964-1980, 2014. $15*
Ted Pearson, *After Hours, 2016, $15*
Andrew Schelling, *A Possible Bag*, 2013, $15.95
Andrew Schelling, *The Real People of Wind and Rain*, 2014, 18.95
Susan M. Schultz, *Dementia Blog*. 2008, $15.00
Susan M. Schultz, *Memory Cards*. 2011, $15.00
Susan M. Schultz, *"She's Welcome to Her Disease*, 2013, **$15.00**

These titles are available online at **www.singinghorsepress.com**, or through Small Press Distribution, at (800) 869-7553 or online at **www.spdbooks.org**